Gazing into the Nest 2

Meet the Eaglets

Stephen A Turner

Contents

Chapter	Page	Subject	
One	5	Nelson	First Year
Two	29	Spirit and No name	Second Year
Three	47	Glory (My name)	Third Year
Four	73	Pictures with the parents	
Five	82	Recent pictures of the parents	

Gazing into the Nest 2: Meet the Eaglets

The following account is in my own words and pictures which I have taken observing a pair of American Bald Eagles and their offspring for the past three seasons. Every major milestone in these birds life from the age of three weeks until around week twenty four will be represented. I do not claim to be an expert on eagles but have witnessed and learned a lot that I am happy to share with you.

You will learn about:

How they are fed, what they eat, and when they can eat on their own

When they discover their wings and start practicing all kinds of takeoff and landing positions

How they prepare for flying by jumping and flapping around the nest and then branching

Time spent exploring as well as playing on the ground

Tree, nest, and ground feedings from the parents

The incredible devotion of the parents and their gentleness at all times to their young

When it becomes time to set off on their own

Branching is jumping or flying up to another branch on the nest tree

Fledging is making the first flight

Post fledge bird is one that has left the nest

Chapter One

The story begins with Nelson already born and roaming about the nest when I first became aware of its location and started taking pictures. It was extremely hard trying to take any picture at first due to me being both nervous and excited at just being in the presence of these magnificent birds. Unfortunately I have no early shots of this bird and only became aware of it around week seven or eight when it was just finding its wings. Even at that time it was very difficult getting clear good shots of the chick due to the location and foliage around the original nest. My plan for this book is to give attention to what each individual bird excelled at and show a little bit of the normal growth stages with each bird. As you can see from one of my favorite encounters with Nelson exploring on the ground, it was a handsome bird here at about thirteen or fourteen weeks old.

Nelson right from the moment I first saw it had found its wings and quickly started trying out different positions and working on getting the strength needed to not only employ its wings from a little to fully opened, but to maintain it when required. Early on it was an extremely active bird in the nest and showed a little bit of aggression from the start.

Nelson the week it found its wings around seven or eight weeks old

One week later already jumping in the nest

I think the reason for the early branching was that the nest provided numerous platforms that were perfect for them all to both jump to and perch on. Nelson excelled at both early on and you would always find it perching alone or sometimes with a parent in the tree but on different branches.

Branches all around and easy to get to

First time wings full out at about eight or nine weeks

Note the branches on three sides within easy reach

For the first time on a regular basis I was able to photograph all three birds coming and going into the nest tree and doing daily activities in and around the nest. The nest was proving perfect for the ongoing perching of both parents and branching for Nelson.

These were taken around eight or nine weeks old

This is when Nelson really started branching

As you can see the left side of the nest was a favorite place to perch for Nelson, it basically only had to step out to it. From this platform he would almost on a daily basis practice all sorts of forms and positions preparing for the next and most important step, flying. Learning to control the wings and gaining the strength to maintain these positions is a required progression for getting to the next level.

The wind is another new obstacle that has to be dealt with

Looking down from thirty or forty feet is an intimidating sight that has to be overcome and mastered to move on to the next level. The apprehension must go away once they take that first giant step knowing that at some point they will be returning to the nest to either get fed from a parent or to rest from an exhausting round trying to improve its flying skills.

Looks almost prehistoric

These were taken at about seven to nine weeks old

The learning and practicing of the various wing (take off) positions it will use the rest of its life never stops and gets refined almost daily. One noted position I see a lot from the parents is what I call the stealth position. This is when they streamline themselves according to the restrictions put on them from either a large branch, being surrounded by foliage, or any restricting obstacle.

Very streamlined

Another
example

Now that the fear is overcome starts the real fun and at times incredibly beautiful and majestic stuff, flying. Nelson went about it full on with reckless abandonment and could be considered very comical and fun to watch every time it went out. The landings at first were usually over or under shot or very thunderous from it leaving a trail of broken branches behind. You wouldn't have to actually see it land only hear the commotion that followed it everywhere it went to know it was around. At the beginning it would always take off and dip down and go to ground where we would find it exploring almost every inch of the eighty-eight acres. Until it left the nest on its own I personally never saw it fly over the water.

I just mentioned the often used stealth mode, but more critical is the need to know when to start retracting its wings and bring them in for a clean landing and at times for a clean take off. The parents we see do this flawlessly every time from years of practice whereas Nelson's landings were more uncontrolled and at times painful to watch. Below Nelson is fully opened and just blasts up out through the branches and vegetation.

But hear it lands in control back on the nest tree

Always the adventurous one, Nelson wasn't afraid to take off from anywhere. The higher the tree the better and forever screaming as it was taking off, or from the ground quietly it would appear out of nowhere and buzz right by you.

From the tall spruce is where it was happiest

Nelson set the bar for being an explorer and spending an extremely large amount of time on the ground compared to the other birds. Whether it would be perched on top of a monument, digging in the mud and sand along the river, walking up and down the grassy hills, or playing by and wading in the river, it had a knack for amusing itself.

From lifting off the ground

Or from a monument

It would take off from anywhere quite skillfully

One of my early most memorable encounters with Nelson was stumbling upon it on the ground after it started flying and leaving the nest. I found it walking across a road and I'm sure a little confused feeling the hard hot surface of the tar under its talons. This was the start of many fascinating days coming across Nelson actively exploring and playing for hours on the ground. These encounters enabled me to get many one of a kind

"KEEPERS".

It looks puzzled

From there the next great adventure was finding the river bank and exploring the water and all it had to offer. This was great because it got to meet ducks, swans, rodents, and all sorts of other creatures. But I think it had more fun just playing in the sand and sewer drain or chewing on sticks and twigs it found on the ground.

It's one huge bird

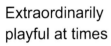

Extraordinarily playful at times

The water seemed to be a safe place for Nelson and besides both playing in and around it she often would perch on the water's edge. Seeing her wade almost up to her wings was fascinating.

It spent hours on the river's edge

Whether it was playing in the sand or just sitting on a log at the river's edge, Nelson felt quite comfortable there and could always keep itself occupied no matter what the weather conditions were or what other creatures happened by at the time.

These next two pictures are appropriate considering that the Eagles have made their home in a cemetery. It appears that nelson is on its knees with its head down reading the inscription and showing great respect in front of the grave marker.

Here it appears to do a fly by

Once out of the nest, Nelson still had to be fed by the parents which led to my next incredible encounter. The feedings were now being done either on a branch in a tree or on the ground in which either one would be both amazing and fun at times to watch. The parent would drop the food and either fly away or perch on a branch nearby.

This is called mantling where the bird spreads its wings covering the food

On a branch with dad along the river

A few more pictures of
Nelson out of the nest

Landing on a monument

These next two are a couple of my favorite pictures of Nelson. The first is when it had just fledged and was becoming quite a little flyer. This big green spruce tree is a favorite of both parents for perching on a perfect summer day or as the tree they use quite often when leaving the area. The

first time I caught Nelson on it the bird opened up fully like it was proud and showing off just before launching mouth wide open screaming the whole time. It was an incredible sight from a bird that young. The second is a great shot of Nelson in the nest just before leaving on its own.

There is not a week that goes by watching the new birds as they are starting out that Nelson's name doesn't come up, usually ending in laughter and a smile. All birds are compared to Nelson but not one yet has measured up to him. The fun and exciting process for us is ever changing both with the new eaglets and the way the parents adopt to each individual bird's strengths and weaknesses. The joy and fun we had watching, hearing, and more importantly chasing and finding Nelson will be hard to match. This picture to me sums Nelson up in a nut shell, adventurous, exploring, a fun loving free spirit that left an indelible mark on all our hearts.

Nelson left the nest for good around the end of September 2016 and was photographed and his tag documented In New York and then not seen again until April second 2017. I was fortunate enough to be there watching the parents working on the nest getting ready for the laying of eggs. I and one other lucky follower in true Nelson manner were alarmed by a sudden crashing of branches and saw him land probably thirty to forty yards from the parent. That was as close as they ever came to each other.

Notice the orange tag with its number meaning Ma. Bird

This was as close as they got to each other

Nelson Update as I'm into the second chapter of the new book. It is September second two thousand eighteen and first year fledge ling Nelson surprised us all by returning to the nest area once again. It was received with great excitement and didn't disappoint seeing the number of serious photographers and others just stopping in the road with an I-Phone snapping pictures. I found him by accident while I was photographing Glory on the ground eating with Nelson perched on a tree very close by in the same area. This being my third year with the birds myself and practically every other follower have never seen a bird that had starting getting its white head feathers.

You can really start to see the changes in the bottom picture, the white roots in the head starting to develop as well as the change from a black beak to a yellow one. At present nelson is approximately two years five

months old. Here is a perfect example how lighting can totally change a picture, is the bird black or brown?

Chapter Two

The second year's chicks started their journey in a new nest in a much better location situated on the river's edge ideal for procuring food and much easier access in all directions. An added and unforeseen bonus to the new location was it enabled me to take and share with you some incredible pictures from within the nest from a hundred yards away. The new chicks, Spirit and No name, where born about a week apart which doesn't sound like much but you could see a remarkable difference in their size and activity levels.

Spirit

No name taken three days later

Eagles have only one brood per year, and replacement clutches can be laid if the eggs are taken or destroyed early on in the incubation cycle. In these two bird's case the first brood was lost due to the nest collapsing and the parents had to go about building a new nest and starting over. These two birds were born in May around Mother's day, about four to six weeks later than the other two chicks. I don't know if this is considered late in the breeding season. Below is my first look at Spirit standing by the Mom about three to four weeks old.

Once the chick has been seen it seems that the feedings come more often around every two hours and we start to see the Mom being able to get away from the nest, even if only for a short while at a time. The meals are usually fish from the river broken up into manageable pieces and beak fed by either parent. The breaking apart of the food by a parent especially when introduced to meat will continue until the sixth or seventh week when

the chick should be able to rip apart the food by itself. In the case of two or three chicks unless there is an abundance of food the older bigger chicks will usually get more.

Hard to see but No name is eating while Spirit looks on

Below is my first picture of the two chicks together taken when Spirit was about four or five weeks old and No name younger by a week. As you can see it is very hard to tell them apart but will get easier as they develop.

Here's Spirit five days later there's quite a change

Here you can see Spirit starting to look like an eagle, the peach fuzz is leaving and he is changing from white to grey feathers. For the next three or four weeks we see a sizeable difference in both height and weight along with an ever changing color of its feathers .

These two pictures of Spirit were taken one day apart

As you can see this is a great time in its development

The following two pictures were taken within a week of each other and you can plainly see Spirit's feathers changing from grey to black. Notice in the first picture with the parent both chicks are about the same size, both between eight and ten weeks old.

Right around this time both birds were taken out of the nest brought to the ground and checked, weighed, and banded by a State Wildlife team. It was quite evident that No name was having trouble keeping its head up and was appearing to have very little energy. Unfortunately within the next week or two it passed. This was devastating to me, all the followers, and I'm sure the parents, after experiencing the old nest collapsing and the loss of the two eggs only a few months ago. Below is the last good picture I was able to take of the bird.

The following picture is the only one in the book not taken by me. It was given to all attendees the day of the banding by the gentleman that went up to the nest. Wish we had his name to give him the credit, he was one brave soul. Notice that for a week's difference in age at this point there's not much difference in size, color, and appearance.

With heavy hearts we continued watching Spirit's development and at that time it was finding its wings, starting to jump, and eventually started branching. In the beginning it would flap its wings as it frolicked around the nest until tired trying to build up its stamina, or simply open up its wings

fully and hold it building up its strength. This process went on for a week or two and led up to its jumping and branching.

Its wings almost look too large for it

Must require a lot of effort just extending and holding the position

Next came jumping at which Spirit really put all its effort into every one and seemed to be a natural right from the beginning. Devastatingly after about a week you began to see a change in its energy levels and becoming a bit lethargic. The jumping around became fewer and less frequent along with the resting for longer periods in between which became the norm

At first watching the bird starting to struggle was a little hard to observe not knowing if something was wrong or if there was a problem, what to do about it. Spirit went on to branching with hardly any noticeable difficulties until it was time to fledge and that's when the real problems started. On its first day out of the nest it ended up on a tree next to the nest tree where it spent the next day or two. That is where the parents fed it while at the same time trying to coax it back up to the nest tree.

This is where it spent its first night out of the nest.

Notice the baby below mantling in anticipation

Dad brought in a fish for breakfast

Unfortunately it ended up on the ground until the next day

I believe it was the very next day that was incredibly hard to stand by and watch without the feelings of utter frustration and hopelessness. The bird started at the bottom of the nest tree and branched all the way up and around the tree to just under the nest while we the followers as well as the parents watched in pain. Looking back I believe that this too was a sign of a looming problem. Spirit did eventually make it back to the nest where I have pictures of future feedings.

Spirit's next week or two was spent dwelling in and around the nest tree on the ground or low in a tree close by. Its flights were always short, usually between two trees in the same area less than half a football field apart. This was not customary activities for a full grown bird which had just

fledged, where normally it should be exploring its new environment. Appearance wise it looked good in the air as well as on the ground but the energy level was never there.

Short flights between two trees

Back in the nest

Spirit's activities became less and less as the days went by. The next several days we found the bird existing on the ground directly below the nest tree with very little movement in the general area. Once in a while you could catch it perched on top of a monument but was never seen in a tree again. The energy just wasn't there! Regrettably Spirit passed and its body was recovered and an autopsy was performed. The cause of death was determined to be a severe infiltration of the liver with trematode flukes. I quote "infected birds usually survive this type of parasitic infection, but the infection was severe for the juvenile eagle. Parents we were told, usually would survive it.

Losing the second bird in such a short time was very disheartening! I like to look at Spirit's life in a positive manner. Yes it was short but it managed to become full grown and incredibly was able to fledge and walk on the ground while sick and struggling before it passed. I like to think No name died of the same ailment without much suffering.

I was only lucky enough to get three good shots of Spirit in the air.

Here is my favorite

This puts to a close a brutal eight to ten months. The collapse of the original nest and loss of the two eggs was tragic, but the loss of the two birds in front of our eyes was very hard to swallow!

Chapter Three

It's a new year as I pine over the last season, still with mixed emotions I watch-over the parents going about breaking branches, grabbing mud and grass, and just getting the nest ready for the upcoming breeding season. After last year I am in need of something encouraging happening over the next forty or so days and I'm anticipating a happy, trouble, and worry free beginning. With great joy and a huge sigh of relief Glory came to us the first week of April, 2018 around a month earlier than last year's two birds. Looking forward to the next twenty weeks I am hoping for both a fun and educational experience without any obstacles or tragedies.

My first sighting and good group of pictures of Glory came between weeks three and four and I was lucky enough to get pictures of it with both parents. I love how you can already see the tenderness and devotion shown towards their new chick and I really have a positive and good feeling about the chick's future. I think it appropriate to put the first picture of the eaglet with the Mom who I've learned is definitely in charge of the nest and what happens around it. For the first time readers you can tell it's the Mom by how huge she is being the bigger parent. I'm showing you the series of first days' pictures because the clarity due to the weather and lack of vegetation or branches around the nest is the best it has ever been.

Here with Dad
the protector

Love
the
peach
fuzz on
the
baby

Let's fast forward about three weeks and we find Glory sitting in the nest about seven weeks old now. You can see the

dramatic color change, difference in size, and it's starting to look like an eagle.

Dad Beak feeding the chick

Now that the baby is about seven to eight weeks old the fun stuff starts. Finding its wings and learning to develop them, starting to flap and jump about the nest, and finally branching and fledging. The time frame for each discipline is different with every bird but the average for all is usually about four or five weeks. Usually the chick will excel at one seeming to almost skip it entirely, or stay on one a little longer. In Glory's case it dragged its feet on jumping, but then blew through branching and the first flight (fledging).

Wing development

Looks great here

Visibly I can't show you flapping which basically is throwing the wings full open and like clapping bringing them together and moving them up and down as the bird is moving around the nest. In Glory's case it seemed like it was stuck on it and jumping and would never branch. When you see the pictures you can see it was quite capable of branching and beyond at an earlier time. Incredibly after the excessive clapping the parents started branching right outside the nest trying to entice it up to a branch outside the nest, even before it started jumping. This went on for many days and then another first when I caught an actual demonstration from the father of branching to the baby.

Here you see the Dad in the nest next to baby jumping up to a branch

Here he jumps back into the nest

He repeated it again before taking off

Next up came jumping which this bird seemed to have

springs under its talons. Glory always got more air time than any bird preceding it and unlike the flapping around it seemed to be in control at all times. Unfortunately like the flapping went on for many days and on many occasions you will see it appeared to be taking off out of the nest.

You can see how it appears to be taking off

Below it appears to be branching but was just jumping and never went to the branch

After about two to three weeks of flapping and jumping around the nest it did finally branch on a limb on the main side of the nest where it still goes out to almost daily.

And finally after a very short time branching, it makes its first flight (fledging). I wasn't in attendance for it but I did get my own first flight from Glory right out the back door (back of nest) and over the river. Right from the start it was a great and powerful flyer that didn't start out with short flights in the local area but long flights out of the area over and across the river. When it returned it seemed to mimic the parents by perching on all the parents' favorite trees when not in the nest. That was one time I didn't mind photographing tail feathers I was just so happy to be there. At the time glory was between twelve and thirteen weeks old.

Here is a few flight shots from within the trees.

 One thing that came up with Glory that was totally out of the norm was that once out of the nest it didn't go to the ground often, only on rare occasions. My first sighting of glory on the ground came about two weeks after its first flight, and even with that I only saw the bird on the ground two or three times after being fed and maybe one or two other times playing.

The first time I came upon Glory on the ground was on a dirt pile in a fenced in construction site when no one was working.

The next time I came upon Glory I found it playing in a puddle of water on the main road blocking traffic.

Like the reflection?

Taking off from the ground, no problem

Look at the wingspan on a sixteen week old bird still developing

Once out of the nest and flying the baby still has to be fed by the parents for a few more weeks until it can hunt on its own. Here's a rare ground feeding

Father drops off the food the baby is mantling over the food

Food is at baby's talons

Baby flies off to a nearby monument to eat

Father stayed perched in a nearby tree while it ate

Another thing I've noticed and learned this season is that the new flyers are very uncomfortable taking off from the very top of the big spruce trees because they are very unstable. On numerous occasions I've observed Glory perched on top for hours enjoying the view and then not knowing quite how to get off the wobbly platform. I've painstakingly watched as the bird opened up and closed its wings over and over again or turned around numerous times only to sit back down again to continue perching. There have been many disappointed onlookers waiting for that perfect takeoff shot only to be disappointed when they see the bird drop down into the lower branches and then take off. What I have noticed over the three seasons is that all the birds usually will perch on a more stable branch on a side of the bigger trees and take off from there. You can see the bend in the top of the tree.

As you just saw you can get a great picture but pack a lunch it'll take a

While!!

I've seen
these
poses from
all the
chicks

As I'm writing this chapter it's the middle of September and Glory is about twenty three or four weeks old now. I never expected it to still be hanging around the nest after seeing the quick start with its flying around the twelfth week. What we have been seeing now is the majority of the feedings by the parents still going on, occur in a tree or in the nest.

The incredible thing I witnessed about this particular feeding was the parent flew into the nest looking around calling for the baby, but was unable to locate it in the area. Dad then took off across the river and I followed it to a tree on a much higher elevation over one hundred fifty yards away to where the baby was waiting to eat. I have mentioned the communication of the birds before while building the nest but this was unbelievable.

I think at this junction an important thing to point out is how the birds are taught to be aggressive when going after food. Whether it's on the ground, in a branch, or in the nest they will push the parents away to get at the food. Here the dad has lunch under his left talon as he braces for the impact. They seem to collide somewhat and the lunch ends up on the ground where the baby recovered it and flew off to eat it and the Dad left the area.

A few more tree feedings for you to see the meat and fish and how well these birds are fed daily.

While it's fresh in mind I'd like to share one more story which happened this morning (9-12-18) while one of the parents was in the area when the baby was getting annoyed at the fact that it hadn't eaten and the parent was perched on a nearby tree. After a short amount of time that I was there (15 mins.) the bird took off and headed for the tree the parent was on and chased it off. Probably for the same amount of time after this the baby kept chasing the parent around tree to tree until the parent left out over the water. At this point the baby returned back to the nest tree to perch and continue crying every now and then for food. Finally the baby Started getting excited seeing the parent flying back in with food heading straight for the nest when it took off and was right on the parents tail feathers as the parent dropped off the food and went to a different tree. The baby ate in the nest and the parent stayed nearby watching over. This is pretty much how it goes for a full grown post fledging Eaglet when their dinner arrives.

This picture shows the bird forcing the parent out

Glory is still on scene so there is no ending this chapter but here are a few more shots of it

Chapter Four   With the Parents

Family portrait   Mom   Glory   Dad

Never saw three
grown eagles
crammed into a nest
before

Family Party!!! 2018

Don't know who the bashful chick is hiding?

Dad always watching over

Fish for
breakfast,
again?

Dad
dropping
in

No idea
what's in
its talons?

Settle down if you want to eat!

Just
leave the
food and
get out!

81

Dad

MOM

Mom

Dad

Always
watching

Coming in
with a
branch

Touching
down

Mom

Dad

Bad or
good
hair
day?

Never
get tired
of the
Mom's
take
offs

She is
gigantic

Dad

Mom

It is now the last week in September, twelve weeks since Glory took its first flight. The parents have tried "tuff" love by staying away for a few days a couple of times hoping the bird would hunt on its own to no avail. If it is hunting it's when away on the daily flights but the parents have been seen still bringing in food to the nest pretty regularly. The bird is still rarely seen on the ground but has blossomed into a powerful flyer with excellent takeoffs and landings. The area around the nest is being thinned out with the removal of over a dozen dead trees all of which the birds have perched on one time or another and some their favorites on an almost daily basis. Happily the birds have adapted to the changes and are going back to trees they haven't used in a long while, but more trees are destined to be removed and I'm hoping they will be back to work next February and getting the nest ready for a great new year.

It has been an amazing three years in which I have witnessed and learned an incredible amount of information about the raising of these chicks and got to see some beautiful and especially tender moments between the chicks and both parents. How the parents adapt to the strengths and weaknesses of each bird is something to behold, and more importantly the never ending patience they show when being the brunt of the aggression from these same chicks when getting slammed on a branch or mauled in the nest over an incoming meal is something to witness. The caring from the parents never stops nor does the learning of the eaglets even after they leave the nest. So now I have some incredible memories of

Nelson our free spirited explorer who spent more time on the ground playing than flying

Glory our best natural and most powerful flyer spending more time flying and chasing the parents around and less time on the ground exploring

Spirit and No name, these two were the first chicks I got to see develop right before my very eyes and will always be my special ones who I humbly dedicate this book to in their memory

So as I Close out this chapter in the birds' story the parents go on with the feedings and Glory seems to be content with staying around the nest (see page 91). I'm sure within the next few weeks it will leave and go off on its own journey but like Nelson I hope it comes back each and every year for a short visit.

Thank you   Steve T   T Z 6 8

Still hanging around the nest

You can see quite a change in its head and appearance

Heading back into the nest

Glory is one week shy of six months old here

Made in the USA
Middletown, DE
08 November 2020